A FAIR RACE

POLICIES FOR A BETTER TOMORROW

TANISHA CHHETRI

For my parents, grandparents, and sisters,

who have loved and supported me in all my endeavors.

Contents

Preface

Two miles away from my house, there is a slum. The lives of these kids living there are very different compared to the kids in my apartment. We're essentially neighbors, but it is like we live in two different worlds. The families living in my apartment could spend the same amount of money in a weekend, that the family in the slum would earn in a year. Wealth inequality is rampant throughout the world. 20 percent of the people own 80 of the world's asset, this is true now and was true even when the Italian economist Wilfred Pareto came up with this in the early 20th century.

Article 26 of the Universal Declaration of Human Rights by the United Nations states, "Everyone has the right to education", this a huge goal that nations strive towards. India has its own version passed in 2009 called the "Right of Children to free and compulsory Education Act", but the implementation of this Act has been a difficult journey, understandably so.

I teach kids aged four all the way to fourteen English and Math (and drawing without which these sessions are incomplete) in that slum. When one of us asked this 8-year-old what he wanted to become, he replied, "Doctor" and immediately a group of boys started making fun of him. This reminded me of how the economist Steven Levitt in his book Freakonomics talks about how when black people study, they are often mocked for "acting white" by those around them. We see these group of boys doing the same thing. It's as if wanting to become a doctor is "acting rich", and when I later asked one of them why he mocked the boy, he just said, "He wants to become a doctor" and laughed again. It was like he had accepted that people from his community couldn't become a doctor, and the thought of it was just absurd. This 8-year-old was made fun of for wanting to become a doctor, something that would seem perfectly normal just one block away. But the glint in that kid's eyes when he said he wanted to become a doctor was what motivated me to write this out, to figure out how one day when another kid in his place says he wants to become a doctor, he isn't shunned or discouraged, but is seen as a normal kid, and encouraged. Someday when this kid won't feel like it is wrong for him to dream of it just because his family is poor.

Ali (name changed), another 12-year-old that I teach has been enrolled in school for a long time but cannot do the three times table. He is still enrolled in school but says that he hasn't gone to school for more than a year now because his school is closed because of the pandemic. Kids who are already lagging behind have been hurt much more by this pandemic. A smart kid who plays cricket in the evening, he says he wants to become like Dhoni. He suffers because he was born into poverty, that is all it is. He is being punished for something that is not even his mistake. There are millions of Alis around India, all in the same boat.

Education undoubtedly has the power to change, not just the life of the individual but also their families, for a generation or more. It has the power to help people get out of poverty, and not just them but also their families through them. We have seen how education changes lives through millions of families throughout India, even my own. I would say that the ripple effects of being educated and escaping poverty is seem throughout the community that these kids belonged to. To the other kids and their parents, it now seems possible to become a doctor, lawyer, engineer, sportsperson, or whatever they want to be, because if this other person who lived near us, and went through the same circumstances as us could do it, so can we. But education is not accessible to everyone, not the same quality of education anyway.

How wealthy your family is, plays a big role in the quality of education that you will receive. The vey problem that education is trying to solve inflicts it. Even though our literacy rates have gone up, we haven't been able to measure the quality of the education that these kids driving up the literacy rates, are receiving. Measuring how the education provided to these kids changes their lives and of those around them is really important, and very hard.

Giving these kids a chance at an equal education compared to the kids receiving in my apartment is important. "Life is a race" is something we have all heard. However, I hope that one day this race has the same starting line for everybody to ensure that all runners have an equal chance to arrive at the same finish line. This book delves into how we could make this possible.

CHAPTER ONE

DOES EDUCATION WORK?

Educations is often regarded as a foundation in all levels, individually, and for society. It powers nations. Through education there is more research, this leads to more innovation, and ultimately a prosperous country with a high standard of living for its citizens. A more education population is good for the individual as well as the society. On an individual level, the individual has access to opportunities, is more productive and will have the skills to fund a comfortable life. For society, a more educated population translates into more innovation, and ultimately productive and highly skilled human capital.

Whether education is correlated to the prosperity of a nation or it is a causation is not very clear. There are various studies conducted and research papers published to support both sides of the debate. But does education work? A look around me would give a positive answer. Although we don't understand the correlation or causation between education and prosperity of a nation, on an individual level, the answer seems clear. Education has the power to give individuals more opportunities, stability, and a higher salary. One person from a family who gets educated, and gets a well-paying job has the power to change the economic status for an entire family for a generation, and more. While being educated opens many doors, and is regarded by a lot of people as the path to success, it also teaches individuals to be better citizens of a country.

Finland has often been revered as the country with the best education system in the world on various metrics. It boasts a literacy rate of 100 percent, a big model for the case of universality of education. Their education system is regularly featured on top in the Programme for International Student Assessment Studies (PISA) studies. The study conducted by PISA compares the reading, science and mathematics abilities of 15-year-olds' in more than 50 countries. In a report by the Ministry of Foreign Affairs of Finland, under the column, "What's our secret?", the first thing mentioned is "Education is a National Priority", highlighting their governmental involvement in this success story. For all the laurels that Finland's education system has acquired, their system always wasn't like this. We can trace the change back to 50 years ago when the Finnish government examined the education system and wanted to implement change. They added better, progressive reforms that would prove to be imperative in the future, although at that time, these changes were untested. These changes implemented from the basic early education stage to higher education level armed students with incremental life skills. Finland is ranked as having the most well-developed education system in the world by World Economic Forum's Global Competitive Study.

Another example of a great education system would be that of South Korea. Boasting a literacy rate of 97.6

percent. In 1962, Sout Korea was incredibly poor with a GDP of a mere $100 per capita. Today it boasts a GDP per capita of $30,000, an economic miracle. After the war, the government developed a highly centralized education system. This system might not be perfect but has worked wonders for the country, injecting millions of highly skilled workers into the workforce.

According to UNICEF, in 2006, there were 14.46 million children out of school in India. This number has dwindled to 6.1 million in 2014. India has been seeing a steady rise in the number of children going to school thanks to various private, and governmental efforts. Although we see these children going to school, the retention rate at school is a crucial number that we should look at to understand how these efforts pan out, and come up with measures to keep children in school.

India has been known for its intellectual prowess, and we often claim with pride how it was in this country that the number zero was invented. But taking a step back makes us wonder, how well are these opportunities distributed? Do the ones who really need it have access towards quality education which will equip them with skills for life? The wealth inequality in India is stark, and this issue seeps through all aspects of life.

The Covid-19 pandemic has affected this even more. Schools have been shut down, both government and private. While some schools offer online classes (mostly private), these kids do not have the means to access these classes being held. They lack the electronic equipments and the internet required. And there are schools which aren't even hosting online classes, with this, even children with phones, laptops, and tablets with internet connection are not even given the choice. This has led to kids seeing school as a thing of the past, somewhere they used to go, and a place they know they aren't going anytime soon.

This has stunted the growth of these kids, with them lagging behind even more than they already did. While teaching, a 10-year-old would have trouble going past the three times table. Another issue that arises with all this free time that the kids have is joining gangs, and getting addicted to drugs or alcohol. Ali (name changed), a 12-year-old kid that I taught, had very yellow eyes. When I asked him what happened, he said it was because of the drugs he was taking. When he told me his age, it struck me that my sister's the same age, but their lives look so different. Ali used to go to school, in fact, he is still enrolled at his local government school. He told me that the school has been shut for months and laughs at the thought of his school every opening.

The universality of education is a great goal that India is striving towards, but it should also keep in mind the quality of the education, and most importantly access to and retention of those kids that need it the most. Let us not chase one metric- literacy rate, and compromise on the other factors that could potentially make the lives of the kids who graduate out of this system, better.

CHAPTER TWO

INCENTIVES

Incentives run the world. When provided an incentive, humans tend to react to it. Incentives have been studied by economists for a long time, and so there is vast literature available on the topic. Incentives for education in India can be divided into two ways. Incentives to help students enroll at school, and to keep these kids at school until they graduate, and incentives to make teaching better at these schools.

Becoming a teacher at a government school in India is a coveted job, much like the country's other government jobs. One would never get fired (unless they do something gravely wrong), so one can do the job casually which usually means just showing up and doing the bare minimum, and once a teacher retires, they are guaranteed pension for the rest of their lives. Some positions come with extra perks like housing, and house help. Therefore, once someone becomes a teacher at a government school in India, their life is considered "set". With no motivation to do a good job, this hampers the teaching environment in schools throughout India.

Sometimes teachers don't even show up to class. And other times, exploiting the loopholes, they somehow manage to register to teach at tens of different schools, not showing up to teach but collecting the salary nonetheless. This description paints a very bleak picture of the situation in Indian Government schools. Not all the teachers at government schools are this way, but quite a large number are. This is due to the accountability problem that arises in these schools.

The teachers are not held accountable for the result of their students or judged by any metric whatsoever. To fire a teacher is, like I've mentioned earlier, almost impossible. They have strong teacher unions, and politicians hold them dearly. Nobody wants to have the teacher unions on the wrong side with elections coming up. Politicians and those in charge respond to the incentive of getting elected or reelected. And teachers, well they do not have any incentive. On top of that, teachers also have various duties assigned that have nothing to do with the classroom. They are held responsible for conducting elections, and educated the area regarding various programs that are funded by the government, or raising awareness about things that the high-ups ask them to.

While some schools have teachers, the others don't even have teachers. India is facing a shortage of teachers, and more so for the already affected government schools. The vacant positions are hard to get filled.

Several countries including the United States compares the performance of their teachers in K-12 education. Conducting research, and collecting data on the performance of these classes would be very valuable in understanding the situation that these students as well as the teachers face. This could also help us uncover the incentives that these students and teachers would react to.

Teachers at government schools also tend to be lesser qualified. Setting a standard of education, and more importantly, providing these teachers with the necessary training could be crucial. The ESEA program in United States is a very good example to look up to in this space. Through this program, the government provides the funding for professional development and instructional materials. Training provided to these government school teachers could also open the door for more teachers to fill the thousands of vacant spots left. With programs such as these, teachers will have the resources to provide quality education for the children who need it the most.

Teachers can also be incentivized for better results by giving them a certain amount of raise that if their students had a higher passing rate in exams. But this would be a tricky concept to apply since a lot of cheating can take place, with teachers inflating the student's grades. For this to work, the students will have to give a centrally or regionally administered exams, which check the skill of the kids according to grades. For example, multiplying 2-digit numbers for grade 2. On top of centrally or regionally administered exams, the crucial part comes when we decide how these exams are graded. These exams should not be graded by teachers from the same school that the child attends, instead it should follow the grading method of the ICSE and CBSE boards, where the exams are shuffled to be graded at random to teachers and schools throughout the country. Another step to take for the prevention of cheating is the environment in which these exams are conducted. They should be conducted in a similar setting to the ICSE and CBSE board exams for 10th and 12th grades, where the exam is invigilated by teachers of another school in the city or region. These preventive methods would help ensure a fair environment for the students to give exams in as well as a correct evaluation of the teachers' efforts.

Offering several incentives based on various metrics obtained from this examination should be effective in providing motivation to these government school teachers, as well a measure of accountability. Giving teachers the right environment and the tools to succeed, makes it easier for the teachers to teach effectively as well.

Incentives for Students

The government in India is using incentives to get children to school. One of its most widely known programs is the Mid-day meal program. This is a very thought-out program which has seen a lot of success. The children going to government schools tend to come from very economically challenged backgrounds, and as the family grows, it gets harder to feed everybody with the nominal wages earned by the parents. Because of this reason, the parents tend to send kids to work after a certain age so that they can help the family financially. Sending their kids to school instead would affect the family because this means one additional mouth to feed without the income that this child brings in. This is where the Mid-Day meal program comes in. Through this program, the children at government schools receive a nutritious lunch, which lowers the burden of feeding one more person in the family. Starvation among these families is not unknown, and knowing that their child gets to eat at least one nutritious meal, provides more incentive for the parents to send their children to school.

But this does not seem to be enough to actually keep these children at school. Even though a record number of children at enrolling at schools, an even more important metric to look at would be the number of children who stay in school. School is essentially an exercise in delayed gratification. Children study, and although learning is a very big benefit, they usually have to wait long enough to see education reap its economical rewards. Wasir, a 14-year-old says that he dropped out of school because he didn't see the point of it. He says that he has already learned the basics and knows how to read and write, and so he would rather work as a mechanic in a small automobile shop and actually earn, rather than "wasting his time" in school. His argument makes sense from one perspective, money is important to him and his family, by working at this automobile shop, he is essentially becoming self-sufficient, and can also help out his family monetarily. So how can we keep children in school and aid them to finish their K-12 education?

A dropout prevention organization in the United States called Communities in Schools (CIS) partner with the nation's schools most vulnerable to dropping out high school students- also called "dropout factories"- and help the kids at these schools graduate high school. They offer academic help, mentoring, clean clothes or just some kind words to those kids whose days got started on a rough note. CIS serves 1.25 million students annually, and out of these kids, 97 percent of potential dropouts stay enrolled and 88 percent on high school seniors graduate in time. Their program costs $200 per student per year. At this cost, it is very hard to actually implement a program of this stature and see the same benefits that CIS has reaped. But we can learn from these programs to try and replicate a similar structure albeit with more pressure on those serving these schools. Keeping at least one person in charge of the students' well-being per grade. Student support is a very important factor. These students are already coming from very challenging backgrounds and need some personal support. This kind of mentoring for the students can do wonders, helping them not give up on school even when it looks like the most sensible thing to do at the moment.

The parents of these kids have to see the possibilities that school unlocks for their children, they also have to believe that their kids can achieve all these things. Recruiting kids who have been able to escape poverty to come to these schools, give them a talk or maybe an exercise, and be an example to these kids to show that that yes, with hard work, this is possible, could go a long way. These parents are often illiterate themselves and cannot understand what their child is being taught at school, let alone advocate for better. In this case, the schools, and people in charge of these schools should take charge.

Introducing a higher paced track for these kids is one way. Emphasis should be put on public schools for those who do well much like a system that New York City has adopted. Highly coveted schools like Stuyvesant High School, are public schools with very high standards of admission. They do not look at family backgrounds but at a test score that the city's kids take in Grade 8 to qualify for these special schools. Each state in India could adopt something similar. With very coveted government schools, and an exam for the admission into these schools. This would motivate the kids to do better, and prepare for these exams, and even if they happen to not get selected, they will still have learned a lot, and the process of learning would teach them a lot. Special schools like these would also provide a platform for these kids who want to do well in school but might not have good opportunities at their local government school. These special schools will have to be schools with options available for boarders since kids throughout the state would be coming here. With free boarding and food, these kids and their parents would have a very high incentive to do well in school to get here. And once here, the environment would help these students strive towards what they are capable of doing but loose out because of their economical background, something that is out of their control.

Similar kinds of programs do exist throughout India but they're all privately run. Shiv Nadar's school provides scholarship to a handful of students from disadvantaged backgrounds. A lot of these kids have graduated high school and gone to top universities and colleges in the world like Cornell University and Babson College, proving that with guidance, resources and opportunities, these kids can achieve great things, and turn around their lives, and that of their families. And it doesn't just end at that, they also inspire those in their communities, and are living proofs of yes, that can happen. But the problem is that these private efforts are not enough, and the government should learn from the models that these private efforts have applied and try and replicate it to success.

Incentives are a powerful way to transform society for the better, and applying incentives to increasing the quality of education for those that need it the most is important. Humans do what they think is best for them, and incentives can guide these students and families to overcome these challenges that they have faced, and alleviate them. Broadly, society with equal educational opportunities is bound to be good for the individual, and society. This means that it benefits the government to work towards this goal, and this should be an incentive for the government to work on making this a reality.

CHAPTER THREE

INFRASTRUCTURE

Savlon, a handwash brand, launched a campaign in some rural Indian schools called Healthy Hands Chalk Sticks campaign. They distributed chalk amongst these kids which was infused with a handwash. The chalk powder that sticks to the kids' hands turns into a later when in contact with water. In these families that tend to starve on days, soap is a luxury, and so children aren't in the habit of washing their hands. This has grave effects. Hindustan Unilever had launched another campaign a couple of years ago called, "Help a Child Reach Five", through which they tried to inculcate the habit of handwashing among children to reduce infant mortality rates. The results from this campaign were a reduction in the rate of Diarrhea from 36 percent to 5 percent.

A lot of government schools lack basic infrastructures such as functioning toilets, classrooms with chairs and tables, or books. A lot of these children write with chalk on chalkboards which comes with its own set of challenges for retention. These children lack the very things that we associate school with, books and pencils. When journalists from Hindustan Times visited Molarbund Boys Senior Secondary School, a government school in South Delhi's

Badarpur, they noticed that the school toilets were stinking from a distance because the two workers hired to clean the toilets were "heart patients who are mostly absent". Drinking water was only available in the Teachers' Staff Room, and the students were not allowed to drink this water since teachers paid for it. The school had only 120 teachers for 7,000 students. A teacher goes on to say that some classes have over a hundred students and the lacking infrastructure of the school means that they have to take classes in the corridors.

There are hundreds, if not thousands of schools like this spread throughout India, hindering the children from learning and the teachers from teaching. School is supposed to be a learning friendly environment for the kids, and not someplace that is always chaotic, with overflowing children, lack of teachers to manage them, or even a lack of space in the school for them to have their desks.

Most prominent schools throughout India boast about their low student to faculty ratio. They pride themselves in being able to provide each child that they take on with ample personal attention. This personal attention often translates into children being more involved in class, and doing better by various metrics such as test scores, passing rates, and class participation. Contrasting that to the government schools in India, the children who are already disadvantaged and have to deal with a lot of pressure from being economically disadvantaged, do not get a proper education, or at least one with quality. While the children at private schools have an environment that is conducive to learning, the children at Indian government schools suffer with an unfavorable learning environment. These children need education much more to level the playing field.

As more kids enroll into government schools with a rising number of children in India enrolling at schools, the school's infrastructure is going to be under more and more pressure. An overcrowded school will not provide these children with the quality education that they need.

The government of India, at the central level has taken measures to fix these issues, but they are nearly not enough. A lot of times, much like any other contract handed out by the government, the winner tends to be in bed with the government, a favored party. From here on, things usually go downhill, the money gets lost between the exchange between different hands, and the schools gets a fraction of the improvement, if any at all. This problem of corruption is not unique to the education system in India, it is rampant throughout. The Modi government has taken many steps to curb this corruption and his government takes pride in taking these steps. But the government schools are still riddled with infrastructural problems.

A solution to this would be to hand out the project in a fare method to the highest bidder, and emphasize on complete transparency in the accounts. Since depending on one set of accountants is a bad idea because of how easily they can get corrupt, the books should be checked by various accountants. The progress of the project, as well as the final product should be checked by those in charge by visiting the site.

When the government outsourced the work for Indian Passports to Tata Consultancy Services (TCS), they did a tremendous job, way better (and faster), than how it had been done before. Handing out these projects to reliable private companies through a fare process and more accountability should be able to accomplish similar results for the education system as well.

Some private companies which have forayed into the space have done a tremendous job. These companies sometimes tie-up with local NGOs to build schools that are run by these NGOs and companies. An example of this would be Rajkumari Ratnvati Girl's School in the rural desert of Jaisalmer, Rajasthan. Architects designed the school in the shape of an oval that can stand temperatures up to 50-degree Celsius, an architectural feat. One kid when asked about the school said, "I feel free here." This school is an example amongst hundreds that have been built for the lesser fortunate thanks to wealthy benefactors, private companies, and NGOs. These schools also stand as proof that infrastructure of the Indian education system for the underprivileged can be improved, and they do affect the lives of these children.

Two toilets for 7,000 kids is inhumane, and on top of that, these toilets are not cleaned regularly, becoming a breeding ground for diseases like diarrhea, and other life-threatening diseases. No kid should be in such a situation. Infrastructure aids these kids' learning and a compromise on infrastructure means a compromise on the future of these kids. These kids who are the future of India, brimming with potential, waiting for someone to given them a chance to succeed.

CHAPTER FOUR

Sports and its Prominence in Education

Play is very important in the development of children. Sports are not only fun but also build character, and help kids stay healthy. Moreover, for some kids, sports might be their talent, and they should be given the opportunity to hone their talent.

Most schools have a PE period, this class looks different in different schools. In some schools, kids might play basketball, in others they might get to run around the track but most schools have understood the importance of this class in the overall development of students, and made it a mandatory requirement for their students. Personally, this was my favorite class in school.

Government schools in rural India lack the basic facilities, and so sports are not very high on their priority list. Some schools promote sports because if their school wins, they get allocated some extra funds which could be used to fix numerous issues in the school. The school can also pride itself in this achievement of winning. PE classes in these schools are essentially a free class where children run around the field without any structure, this is fine sometimes. But these schools also lack sports programs. What if someone wants to become a great cricket player like Sachin Tendulkar? Keeping in mind that these kids live in rural areas, they would not have access to any cricket facilities in the region. In cases like these, their schools become crucial for these kids because they have the ability to teach these kids, and could very well be their only hope.

Rajan Singh, an ex-IPS officer wrote about how the coaching centers for IITJEE have a network of middlemen who hunt down students so that the other coaching centers cannot get their hands on these kids first. He goes on to say that if we had such an efficient system for searching for talented players, India would beat China at the Olympics. India's focus on sports is undoubtedly growing, but this growth should not be concentrated just in cities, or places with more influence. These kids from rural areas also should be given a chance. If a system like the coaching system for JEE works, then so be it.

There is a famous saying which goes like talent is universal but opportunity isn't. Giving these opportunities to kids is very important, and could potentially change their lives. There are various examples of a similar kind of story that we can see in Sportsmen throughout India. Most of these people came from humble backgrounds, and went on to become great players, and in some cases, even household names through their hard work. Hardik Pandya, Mary Kom, and even Sachin Tendulkar have achieved great things in the field of sports and transformed the lives of their family members along with them. Their rise also inspired kids, and showed them that no matter your background, with hard work anyone can reach that level of greatness. But to even get started, these kids need a little backing, a bit of lift-off, and it should be our responsibility to give them that.

CHAPTER FIVE

"Padhegi Beti Toh Badhega Desh"

While India has come a long way in terms of equality of gender, we are still quite not there yet. In parts of India when a girl child is born, it is still considered a burden. Some families consider killing this child or just leaving this girl child in a dumpster. Therefore, it comes as no surprise when the education of girls is not given a very high priority.

In some rural parts of India, the thought of "why should she be educated when she has to get married off?" still exists. A daughter is seen almost like a guest for a few years, like she doesn't belong to the family since she will have to get married and will eventually join another family. And so, the literacy rates of girls are far lower than that of boys, especially in rural areas. There are a lot of concerns families have regarding sending their daughters to study in schools.

Another concern would be boys mingling with girls in these schools. Families think about what kind of an environment will their daughter be in with boys all around her. They are concerned about how the presence of boys all around them would affect their character. Then there is always the question of these girls ending up falling for their classmates. As marriage is seen as the ultimate goal of a daughter's life, how would the potential groom's family think about their future daughter-in-law being surrounded by all these boys.

A big reason that girls who end up enrolling at schools have to drop out is because of puberty. Once a girl starts menstruating, her family tends to make her drop out of school. This happens due to various reasons. In some communities, periods are still seen as a taboo, and girls who are menstruating are not allowed to see anyone or touch anything because they are considered "impure." Confined to a room or some designated area, they are left with no choice. Hitting puberty is also when a female transitions from a girl to a "woman" causing families to be more conscious of their daughters for various reasons. Mostly these reasons are tied to getting a groom.

Then there is the concept of child marriage. Once they are considered women (sometimes even younger), they get married to someone who is generally years older than them, and "sent off" to become a part of another family. Once married, these girls can only dream of going to school as they get busy in their married life.

Infrastructural challenges that these government schools face also contribute to this issue. With not many functioning toilets available, and more importantly, these girls lacking sanitary pads, it becomes hard for them to go to school. Sanitary pads are a luxury, a fact that shines through the "luxury tax rate" that was formerly imposed on it. Many NGOs are working towards providing sanitary pads, so that these girls do not have to drop out due to this reason.

The government of India has also launched various programs raising awareness regarding the education of girls like "Beti Padhao, Beti Bachao", and another famous tag line, "Padhegi Beti Toh Badhega Desh."

While these programs are providing good incentives for the families to send their daughters to school. Schools in the districts can also raise awareness camps and incentive these families to send their daughters to school, showing them that marriage is not the end goal of a girl's life, and that they can also be the bread winners of these families, and bring the family as much pride as a son would.

CHAPTER SIX

LEVERAGING TECHNOLOGY

According to a UNESCO 2021 State of the Education Report for India, only 19 percent of schools in India had access to Internet. This is private and government schools combined. Government schools lack basic amenities like washrooms, and so the internet is a long shot for them.

The power that technology has unlocked in terms of education is immense. The internet has enabled people to get information on anything they want within minutes at their fingertips. The most well-known teacher is Sal Khan, the founder of Khan Academy, an online learning platform. Today, anyone can take a class taught at Harvard or Stanford for free, from anywhere around the world with a stable internet connection. The effects of this are enormous.

I started this book by comparing the privileged children in my apartment with those who do not share the same kind of privilege. But technology has the power to make this field of education a level playing field. Thanks to Jiofication in India, internet has become very cheap, and India has had astronomical smartphone adoption. A blue-collared worker who works for my apartment has a daughter, Asha (name changed). One day, while playing tennis, I heard her talk and was surprised. She spoke English way better than the other kids in my apartment. Hell, she even had a mix of an American, Australian, and a British accent. I was stumped, and so were others who heard her speak. Some kids in my apartment could not reply back as they didn't understand what she was trying to say. Knowing how to speak English in India has long been seen as a privilege, maybe it was because we got colonized or because English is the language of the West, not a lot of people knew how to speak English. But thanks to the miracle of YouTube, and Peppa Pig and Paw Patrol, learning English is becoming a level-playing field, increasing its access.

Sal Khan has a vision for the world's school to be enabled by the internet, anywhere around the world, no matter the background of the kid, as long as they have an internet connection, they can get access to world-class education. The internet is a powerful thing. It is democratizing education, making it more accessible for children like Asha to not only learn English, but whatever they want to learn. This kid learned a whole new language, a language that her parents do not know, by herself, at around 8 years, that, to me, is incredible. Providing a bit more structure to the learning environment and altering the way these kids use technology can be the dark horse that we have been hoping for all this while to make this a fairer society.

The best part about the internet is, how easy it is to scale. Investors love internet businesses for this reason. They can build a product once, and sell it multiple times. A lot of private effort has been put into making the education system in India better, but often private methods are hard to scale throughout India. Technology can enable this. A private effort into this field would effectively scale. The government of India can also come up with curriculums or standards for online learning.

Technology has disrupted every single industry. Using technology's leverage to fix the education system might just be the dark horse we have all been hoping for.

CHAPTER SEVEN

THE SECRET WEAPON: NGOS AND PRIVATE COMPANIES

Non-governmental Organizations (NGOs) and Private Companies have set up various schools, and initiatives that have made the lives of the less fortunate better. The role that they have played is uncontested because of the impact that they have had. These organizations also provide a high quality of education. The only problem that these efforts face is that of scale. To scale their offerings requires large amounts of investments, money that they try hard to raise but isn't enough to reach every child affected.

One day I was scrolling desperately through Netflix, searching for something to watch before my food got cold. I came across a suggestion, "Daughters of Destiny." The preview was very intriguing and I started watching it, soon my sisters joined me, and in some time, my mother, grandmother, father, sisters and I were hooked. The documentary took us through the lives of five families' whose daughters had been selected to be a part of the Shanti Bhavan Children's Project. Started by Dr. Abraham George, an Indian-American philanthropist, this initiative selects 24 preschool kids, and provides them with free education and boarding till the 12th grade. Children who want to pursue higher education also receive support while pursuing their degrees. The documentary was shot over the course of seven years, and shows us the intricacies of these families' lives. The pressure on the girls does not go unnoticed, but this chance that they receive is undoubtedly life altering for not just the kids who get selected but also for their families. The Shanti Bhavan graduates have gone on to work at various multinational companies like Amazon, Deloitte, and Ernst and Young. These graduates are also grateful for the opportunity that they were provided, and often give back to this initiative in various ways.

What Dr. Abraham George has done has also created also has a ripple effect. Through the documentary, we also see how these kids impact the lives of those around them. From their families to the communities that they live in. One of the girls, actually going on to find a lawsuit against a mining company because that land belongs to her people.

Another example of this would be VidyaGyan, an initiative by the Shiv Nadar Foundation. In this program, underprivileged children are picked based on an exam. VidyaGyan has had various alumni enter the civil services and Indian Defense forces. Their students have also gotten full scholarships to world renowned universities. Anurag Tiwari from UP, a farmer's son, recently won a full scholarship to Cornell University, and is currently studying Economics and Mathematics there.

Various other private companies like Infosys and Tata Industries have done a lot of meaningful work which has changed the lives of these children. India's Corporate Social Responsibility is also a contributing factor, a great step that the government has taken. These private companies have embraced and this has led to a lot of good work.

The role that NGOs and Private companies play has been crucial in the education space. The government has also done a great job at supporting these organizations.

Indian Institute of Technology

There are various locations of Indian Institute of Technology (IIT) now, but it all started with a dream to bring expertise, research and development to India. To make the workforce competent and skilled. This has expanded to a great network throughout India, Institutions providing world-class education.

Going to IIT is a matter of great privilege for any India. Once you've made it, your life is going to be great. This dream of academic excellence has made it very difficult to get into IIT, a fact that has only increased its prestige. When compared statistically, it is harder to get into IIT than it is to get into Harvard University. Every year millions of kids prepare for the Joint Entrance Exam (JEE), all hoping to crack it, and finally realize their dream.

Kids start preparing for IIT since 6th grade or even earlier. This emphasis of preparation, and getting the best of preparation, has given birth to an entire industry. There a town called Kota, known to be a hub of preparation for all these aspirants. For some aspirants, this is all they can think of, their lives are dedicated to perfecting their knowledge for this exam.

The low acceptance rate also means that every year millions of these kids are heartbroken. After dedicating years to this one exam, they are not able to crack it. These years that these kids dedicate is a significant portion of their young lives, sacrificing everything, a huge exercise in delayed gratification.

But for those who do get in, they've hit jackpot. They get the best opportunities, and education that India has to provide. Once somebody has the "IIT tag", although they will still have to work hard, the tag will definitely make a few heads turn, and make it easier to notice these bright women and men.

70 percent of India's CEOs are from IIT, and 60 percent of the unicorn founders in India are from IIT. These are staggering numbers. For a group that represents less than 5% of the white-collar workforce, their alumni seem to be doing very well. Not just in India, but alumni from the IITs have gone on to become CEO at Google, and found great firms like Khosla Ventures. Their influence on the world has been great.

The IITs are on a quota system, and this allows kids a push that was needed for them to get here. IITs are the pinnacle of meritocracy, if you want to get in, there is only one way- to crack the Joint Entrance Exam. And in my opinion, it is this meritocracy that shines through the alumni of these Institutes.

India's visionary leaders created these great educational institutions to benefit India, and the world. This vision has been realized with these institutes doing ground-breaking work, and the people who graduate from here making the world better. They have stood as pillars of pride in our education system, proving our ability to build world-class institutions. The excellence of IITs should seem through all levels of education in India.

CHAPTER NINE

Kerala: A Case Study in Literacy

Kerala, a State in Southern India, has been boasting the highest rates of literacy in India for a long time now. Their literacy rate was 96.2 percent in 2021, 18.5 percent more than the national aggregate which stood at 77.7 percent. Kerala has been leading in terms of education for a long time now. They have been closer to the literacy rate of Finland than to the other Indian States. So, how did Kerala achieve this feat?

The quest for universal literacy in Kerala began in the 19th Century. The Queen of Trivandrum issued a royal decree which made education free in 1817, it said, "The state should defray the entire cost of education of its people in order that there might be no backwardness in the spread of enlightenment." This incredible foresight of their ruler set the stone rolling for the state. They still benefit from this foresight. Later, the other rulers of the region like the King of Cochin took charge by setting up public schools, and promoting elementary education. The Christian missionaries furthered this mission by setting up schools for people with all castes and backgrounds, breaking down the barrier set for people who belong to less fortunate backgrounds, since at the time, the tradition was that of only high-class Indians attending schools.

This rich history, and promotion of education for centuries has helped education be cemented as a high priority among the people of the state. Because of this, the State government of Kerala has emphasized its priority in this field to a great extent. A significant portion of the State's budget is allocated to education. Kerala also boasts a large network of Public Libraries, especially in the rural areas thanks to PN Panicker's Library Movement. The people of Kerala regard education in the utmost level, and want to educate their children as much as possible.

However, the literacy rate does not reflect the performance of the economy of the state. Primarily an agrarian state with a per capita income of $3,300 (in 2020-2021), the state has a high unemployment rate, even higher than the average unemployment rate in India. There isn't much investment or business development in the state, and so, there are very few jobs. This makes us question whether a high literacy rate translates to a better economy, or better job prospects for those getting educated.

Kerala's higher education institutions also lag behind their peers at other states. They lack infrastructure, and are also behind in terms of research. Their engineering and medical universities are of low quality.

Although looking at Kerala, this education does not entirely go without any effect. A large population of Kerala goes to work in other states, the Middle East, United States, and other countries throughout the world. The money that these workers send back home is a major contribution to

Kerala's economy, some even go so far as to calling it the "backbone" of Kerala's economy. These people are able to find these jobs thanks to the quality of education that they receive in their formative years of schooling. This is an important factor in making Kerala's literacy rate a chief asset to the state.

CHAPTER TEN

GOING FORWARD

India's economy is growing rapidly. The investment in the economy is increasing with each passing year from domestic institutions as well as international institutions. There is no doubt that India is well on its to way to become a top economy of the world. But let us not leave anyone behind, especially the less fortunate.

The Right to Education Act passed in 2009 was a huge move for the nation, a step forward for the kids that most need education. This free and compulsory education policy has done a lot for the future of these kids and increased their access to getting an education, no matter their background.

But India should not just focus on literacy rates for these kids, the impact that quality education has on the lives of these kids, and a nation as a whole could be immense. Setting up different metrics can help us measure the quality, and give us a trove of data to analyze how education policies can be altered to optimize for quality. As we have seen in the case of Kerala, universal literacy is a great goal with a lot of impact, but have a high quality of universal literacy could be a game changer for the nation, and for these kids.

Moreover, hiring and training teachers is a huge measure that we should optimize for. A good teacher has the ability to change the lives of hundreds of students, not just in class but even outside of class. For this, we have to increase the incentives for teachers. As we have seen in the private sector, a higher salary attracts more talent. Teachers should be given an opportunity to negotiate their salaries, and should be rewarded monetary and through promotions for their students' performance.

The disparities in wealth are a common theme throughout the world but seems especially bad in India. And education is a silver bullet, in terms of growing the economy and trying to lessen this gap in income and wealth. India's huge youth population is the nation's greatest asset, and a skilled youth would only accelerate this progress.

But the very problem that education aims to solve, hinders it from doing so. The potential of each kid is immense, and they should all be given an equal chance to succeed, not be reprimanded for the economic status in the society instead.

I wrote this book to better understand how to bridge the gap in quality education for the kids that most need. My experience teaching these kids has contributed a lot to this endeavor. A thought that crosses my mind often is that I won the lottery of being born to a economically stable family. This arbitrary thing makes a huge difference in the lives that people live. My teacher once told my class about how important money is for people by telling us how we are treated differently from the daily wage workers on the streets by the police. We need to bridge this gap, provide more people with a chance to live a respectful and comfortable life. Let's strive towards an India where a 6-year-old from a disadvantaged background will not be shamed for wanting to become a doctor.